CENTRAL MIDDLE SCHOOL

4283271106

940.54 ADA

Adams, Simon,
The Eastern Front

Documenting World War II

The Eastern Front

Simon Adams

Central Middle School
Media Center

rosen publishing's
rosen
central®

New York

Published in 2009 by The Rosen Publishing Group Inc.
29 East 21st Street, New York, NY 10010

Copyright © 2009 Wayland/The Rosen Publishing Group, Inc.

All rights reserved. No part of this book may be reproduced in any
form without permission from the publisher, except by a reviewer.

First Edition

Editor: Camilla Lloyd
Consultants: Dr. R. Gerald Hughes and Dr. James Vaughan
Designer: Phipps Design
Maps: Ian Thompson
Picture researcher: Kathy Lockley
Indexer and proof-reader: Patience Coster

Picture Acknowledgments: The author and publisher would like to thank the
following for allowing their pictures to be reproduced in this publication:
Cover photographs: BL: AKG-Images, BR: ©Ullstein Bild/AKG-Images;
AKG-Images: 1, 6, 9, 16–18, 26–32, 36–38, 41–42; ©Bettman Archive/Corbis: 39;
Getty Images (Hulton Archive): 4, 10, 14, 34, 35; Mary Evans Picture Library: 11;
©Time & Life Pictures/Getty Images: 19; ©Ullstein Bild/AKG-Images: 5, 43, 44;
©Underwood & Underwood/Corbis: 7, 23.

Library of Congress Cataloging-in-Publication Data

Adams, Simon, 1955-
  The Eastern Front / Simon Adams. -- 1st ed.
      p. cm. -- (Documenting World War II)
  Includes bibliographical references and index.
  ISBN 978-1-4042-1862-8 (lib. bdg.)
  1. World War, 1939-1945--Campaigns--Eastern Front. I. Title.
  D764.A4393 2008
  940.54'217--dc22
                                        2007041461

Manufactured in China

CONTENTS

Hitler and the east

The Eastern Front was the setting for conflict in central and Eastern Europe during World War II (WWII), which lasted from the invasion of Poland in September 1939 until the defeat of Germany in May 1945. The front was notorious for the destruction and loss of life that occurred in countries along its borders. This book will outline what happened on the Eastern Front during the war and its significance in the eventual defeat of Germany.

In January 1933, a new leader took power in Germany. His name was Adolf Hitler, and he led the National Socialist German Workers' Party, commonly known as the Nazis. For the next 12 years, Hitler and the Nazis ruled Germany, turning it into a powerful military state that came to dominate all of Europe during WWII, from 1939 to 1945.

The Nazi Party was formed as the German Workers' Party in 1919 and changed its name a year later. Hitler was its seventh member to enrol and soon became its leader. The Nazis

remained a small party throughout the 1920s, but grew in strength as the German economy collapsed during the worldwide economic depression of the early 1930s. Millions of unemployed people looked to Hitler to rescue their country from poverty and restore German greatness. After months of economic and political turmoil, President Hindenburg asked Hitler to

The Nazi Party staged huge rallies at Nuremberg in southern Germany each September from 1923 to 1938. The rallies were propaganda exercises designed to show the power of the party and every rally ended with a major policy speech by Hitler.

form a new government in the belief that he was the one man who could run the country. Once he was in power, Hitler became a dictator and began to transform Germany.

Hitler set out his beliefs in a book he wrote in prison during 1924. On November 8–9, 1923, the Nazis had tried to seize power in Munich, capital of the southern state of Bavaria. They then planned to march on the German capital, Berlin, and set up a Nazi government. Hitler was imprisoned for five years for his part in the "Munich Putsch," as it was known. He used his time in prison to write *Mein Kampf* ("My Struggle" or "My Battle").

In this book, Hitler set out his hatred of both communism and the Jews. He believed that the Soviet Union— the world's main communist state at that time—was involved in an international conspiracy with the Jews to take over the world, and that the Soviet Union formed the greatest threat to Germany's existence. He also set out his belief that Germany needed *lebensraum* ("living space") in the east in which to expand. He believed the Germans were an "Aryan" (light-skinned, fair-haired) master race who should dominate the world. The people of Eastern Europe—the Slavs of Russia and Poland, and above all, the Jews—were inferior and could be swept away or killed to make room for Germans. Once in power, Hitler set about putting his beliefs into practice.

SOURCE

BOOK

"We are … turning our eyes toward the east … when we speak of new land in Europe today, we must principally bear in mind Russia and the border states subject to her. Destiny itself seems to wish to point the way for us here."

Hitler made very clear in his political statement, *Mein Kampf*, written in 1924, the nature of his ultimate intentions toward Eastern Europe.

Adolf Hitler in *Mein Kampf*, published in 1925.

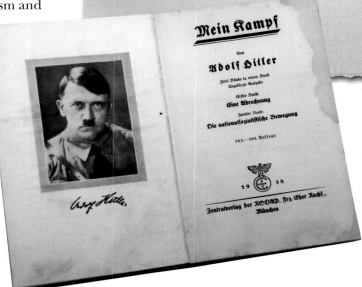

Preparations for war

Between 1914 and 1918, Germany had fought and lost World War I (WWI). The terms of the postwar peace treaty signed in Versailles, outside Paris, in 1919 were harsh. Germany was forbidden to re-arm and had to pay huge "reparations" (war damages) to Britain, France, and other victorious nations. It lost land in the east to Poland, Czechoslovakia, and Lithuania, as well as two western provinces to France and all of its overseas colonies. Hitler came to power promising to scrap the treaty.

As chancellor (prime minister) of Germany, Hitler rapidly built up the German armed forces. In 1936, he sent troops into the demilitarized Rhineland, and in March 1938, achieved *Anschluss,* or union, with Austria. These three actions had been expressly forbidden by the Treaty of Versailles. He built up German industry so that it could produce arms,

The Nazi occupation of the Sudetenland after the Munich Agreement of September 1938 (see page 7) stripped Czechoslovakia of its border defenses and left it vulnerable to future German aggression.

ammunition, and other war materials. Abroad, Hitler formed an alliance with Italy—the "Rome-Berlin Axis"—in October 1936, and signed the "Anti-Comintern" (anti-communist) Pact with Japan the following month against their mutual enemy, the Soviet Union. Italy joined this alliance the next year.

Opposition to Hitler's moves by Germany's former enemies, Britain and France, had been minimal. The leaders of both countries believed that Hitler was right to overturn the harsher parts of Versailles and sought to appease, or pacify, him by agreeing to his demands. In this way, they hoped to avert a future war with Germany.

The test of their appeasement policy came in summer 1938, when Hitler demanded that the heavily industrialized Sudetenland region of Czechoslovakia be brought under German control. When Czechoslovakia objected, Germany threatened war. The prime ministers of Britain and France met with Hitler and the Italian leader, Mussolini, in Munich in September. The Czechs were not invited. The four countries agreed that Germany could seize the Sudetenland. The agreement also gave the Teschen district to Poland and part of Slovakia to Hungary. The four countries promised to guarantee the new frontiers against further aggression.

Many people thought that the "Munich Agreement" guaranteed, as the British prime minister, Neville

Chamberlain, put it, "*peace for our time.*" Hitler, however, believed that the western nations would not oppose him in the future, and so turned his attentions to the east.

The British prime minister, Neville Chamberlain, returned from Munich in September 1938 believing he had achieved a long-lasting peace in Europe.

SOURCE

SPEECH

"… there has come back from Germany to Downing Street peace with honor. I believe it is peace for our time."

The Munich Agreement was greeted by many at the time as a major achievement.

Prime Minister Neville Chamberlain, speaking from Downing Street, London, September 30, 1938.

The threat to Poland

Within six months of the Munich Agreement, the policy of appeasement had failed. On March 15, 1939, German troops invaded what was left of Czechoslovakia. The western half of the country was absorbed into Germany (as the protectorate of Bohemia-Moravia) and the eastern half—Slovakia—became a "puppet" or client state, in theory independent but in fact dependent on Germany.

SOURCE

SPEECH

"… in the event of any action which clearly threatened Polish independence and which the Polish government accordingly considered it vital to resist with their national forces."

British Prime Minister Neville Chamberlain's pledge to protect Poland in a speech on March 31, 1939.

Germany's ally, Hungary, invaded and annexed Ruthenia, a province to the east of Hungary. One week later, Hitler seized the Lithuanian port of Memel, taken from Germany under the Versailles Treaty. He then turned his attention to Poland.

Under the Treaty of Versailles, Poland had regained the independence it had lost in 1795 to Russia, Austria, and Prussia (the forerunner of modern Germany). It also gained a corridor of land—the "Polish corridor"—through Germany to the Baltic Sea. The previously German port of Danzig had become a free city under international control. Both of these were meant to give Poland economic security by allowing it access to the Baltic, but Poland had developed a rival port, at Gdynia, as its outlet to the sea, depriving Danzig of much-needed trade and income. To complicate matters, both the Polish corridor and Danzig had sizeable German minority populations, while Danzig itself was dominated by a local Nazi government. The whole area was therefore a source of much contention between Germany and Poland. On March 21, 1939, Hitler demanded the return of Danzig, and the formation of a link across the Polish corridor between the two parts of Germany, which would cut off Poland from the coast. Poland promptly rejected both demands.

By now, both Britain and France had realized that appeasement would not work against Hitler. On March 31, 1939, the two governments pledged to come to Poland's assistance if it was

The port of Danzig had a substantial German population. Hitler's demand that it be returned to Germany became a cause of the outbreak of war.

attacked by Germany. After Germany's ally, Italy, invaded the Balkan state of Albania in April and with Germany appearing to threaten other countries in the region, Britain and France extended their pledge to Greece and Romania. Both countries stepped up their military preparations. Britain introduced conscription (compulsory military service) for men between 20 and 21 and prepared for war. Plans were made to evacuate women and children from British cities, gas masks were issued, and rationing of food and other items was considered.

Hitler now faced a dilemma. If he invaded Poland, he risked fighting on two fronts, since Britain and France would attack Germany from the west while his troops were fighting in Poland in the east. He decided to continue in Poland, but also to turn his attention to the Soviet Union.

9

The Nazi-Soviet Pact

On paper, Germany and the Soviet Union were complete opposites in their political beliefs and culture. Germany was the world's only Nazi state, the Soviet Union the world's main communist state. Nazi belief was founded on a hatred of communism. For Germany to thrive, the communist Soviet Union had to be defeated. The communists likewise hated Nazi beliefs.

Yet the two countries had much in common. After its defeat in WWI, Germany had become an international outcast. The Soviet Union—which had left the war in early 1918 and played no part in the Versailles peace treaty—was also an outcast. Both felt excluded from the international community. It therefore seemed logical for them to conclude a treaty at Rapallo in Italy in 1922 to establish diplomatic relations and begin economic cooperation.

The Nazi-Soviet Pact was signed in Moscow. The Russian foreign secretary, Vyacheslav Molotov, is shown here with the German foreign secretary, Joachim von Ribbentrop, in the far left of the picture and Josef Stalin, the Soviet leader, is in the middle. The other two men are diplomats.

Although Stalin, the Soviet leader, feared Germany's intentions and wanted closer links with Britain and France, he could not persuade either country to ally with him. Both were anti-communist and had excluded the Soviets from their discussions with Hitler at Munich. Stalin concluded that Britain and France wanted a deal with Germany that would ultimately threaten the Soviet Union. He also concluded that they would not go to war over Poland. He did not want to support Poland only to find his country fighting alone without British or French support. From the German point of view, Hitler needed to make sure that if he attacked Poland, he would not have to face the Soviet Red Army.

It made sense for the Soviet Union and Germany to reach some sort of agreement. On August 23, 1939, the two foreign ministers—Ribbentrop for Germany and Molotov for the Soviet Union—signed a nonaggression pact in Moscow. The public part of the document stated that each would remain neutral if the other was at war. The private part gave Germany a free hand in western Poland and Lithuania, and the Soviet Union a free hand in eastern Poland, Finland, Estonia, Latvia, and eastern Romania. A second secret agreement signed on September 28 gave Germany more land in Poland; in return, the Soviet Union gained Lithuania.

CARTOON

The French satirical magazine, *Le Rire* ("The Laughter"), showed both Stalin and Hitler as bloodthirsty tyrants, although in the illustration above, Hitler looks more worried than Stalin about the unholy pact. Stalin actually believed that the Nazi-Soviet Pact worked in his favor and said to Khrushchev, the future leader of the Soviet Union: *"I know what Hitler's up to. He thinks he has outsmarted me, but actually it is I who have outsmarted him."*

Source: *Le Rire*, 1939.

The world was stunned by this agreement between the Nazis and the communists. The agreement gave the Soviet Union valuable time to prepare for a future war, and Hitler, the green light to invade Poland.

The invasion of Poland

At 4:45 a.m. on September 1, 1939, the guns of the German battleship *Schleswig-Holstein*—paying a "courtesy visit" to Danzig to honor the German war dead of WWI—opened fire on the fortifications commanding the inner harbor of the city. At around the same time, German *Stuka* dive-bombers attacked Polish airfields while German troops dismantled border posts. The Nazi leader of Danzig, Albert Forster, proclaimed the city's union with Germany. The German invasion of Poland had begun.

Although the Poles were prepared, their ill-equipped forces were no match for the five German armies with more than 1.5 million troops that attacked from the north and west. The Germans fought a new kind of war known as *Blitzkrieg*—"lightning war"— in which tanks, aircraft, and motorized infantry combined to attack the enemy at top speed and break up the mass of troops into small, easily attacked pockets.

The effect was overwhelming. By September 16, German troops had begun an 11-day siege of Warsaw; a day later, Soviet troops poured over the eastern border to grab their share of the country. The two armies met on their agreed frontier on September 21. There was some concern that the pact might not hold and that the two armies would fight each other, but each drew up along the new frontier and settled down to cooperate uneasily. Hitler continued the pretence of friendship he had agreed in the Nazi-Soviet Pact, even sending a congratulatory telegram to Stalin on his 60th birthday on December 21, 1939, with best wishes *"for the happy future of the friendly people of the Soviet Union."* By early October, Polish resistance had ended and the country was divided in two.

The response of Britain and France was immediate. After Germany had refused to stop its invasion and

LETTER

"There is hardly a building not in some way damaged. … The people must have suffered terribly. For seven days there has been no water, no power, no gas, and no food."

The damage to Warsaw from the siege by German troops was immense.

Brigadier (later Field Marshal) Erwin Rommel, writing to his wife on October 2, 1939 about Warsaw, Poland.

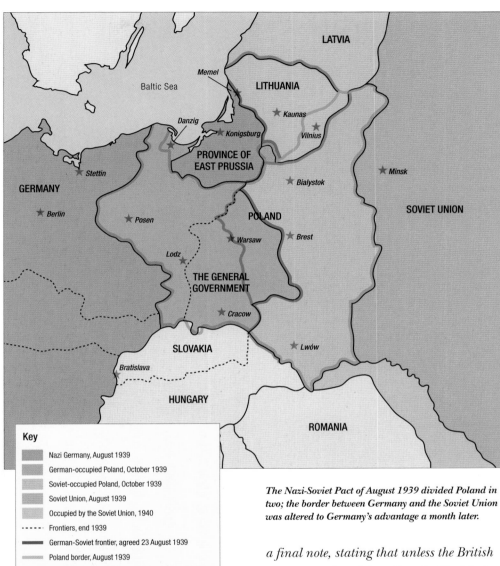

Key

	Nazi Germany, August 1939
	German-occupied Poland, October 1939
	Soviet-occupied Poland, October 1939
	Soviet Union, August 1939
	Occupied by the Soviet Union, 1940
-----	Frontiers, end 1939
	German-Soviet frontier, agreed 23 August 1939
	Poland border, August 1939
	German-Soviet frontier, modified September 28, 1939

The Nazi-Soviet Pact of August 1939 divided Poland in two; the border between Germany and the Soviet Union was altered to Germany's advantage a month later.

withdraw its troops, the British prime minister, Neville Chamberlain, broadcast to the nation on Sunday, September 3:

"This morning the British ambassador in Berlin handed the German government a final note, stating that unless the British government heard from them by 11 o'clock that they were prepared to withdraw their troops from Poland, a state of war would exist between us. I have to tell you that no such undertaking has been received, and that consequently this country is now at war."

World War II had begun.

The Tripartite Pact

After the invasion and division of Poland, the remaining parts of the Nazi-Soviet Pact soon fell into place. The Soviet Union quickly signed military agreements allowing it to station troops in the three Baltic states of Estonia, Latvia, and Lithuania, before occupying all three countries in June 1940.

these moves, the Soviet Union had extended its territory westward, but now shared a long border with Germany.

For its part, Germany took the opportunity to knock out its enemies in the west so that it could eventually face the Soviet Union without fear of being attacked from the east. After a

The Tripartite Pact was signed in Berlin on September 27, 1940 between Italy (left), Germany (center), and Japan (right). Five Balkan countries signed the pact later, although Yugoslavia quickly changed its mind and withdrew its support.

To the north, the Soviet Union launched the "Winter War" against Finland in order to better protect its access to the Baltic Sea.

Despite its successes, the failure of the Soviet Union to achieve a decisive victory revealed massive weaknesses in the Red Army. To the south, the Soviet Union seized two northeastern provinces from Romania. As a result of

rapid invasion of Denmark and Norway in April 1940, Germany attacked the Low Countries and France. When France surrendered in June 1940, Britain and its empire alone remained in the war. At first, Hitler intended to invade Britain, but for that he would need to defeat the Royal Air Force (RAF). Then a massive German invasion fleet could cross the English Channel without fear of an aerial attack. The Battle of Britain, between the Royal Air Force and Germany's *Luftwaffe*, raged from July to October 1940. German *Dornier* bombers escorted by *Messerschmitt* fighter planes attacked British airfields and ports but were, in turn, attacked by British *Hurricane* and *Spitfire* fighters. Day after day, the battle raged across the skies of southern England until the RAF gradually won control. In October, the *Luftwaffe* called off its campaign and focused on trying to bomb Britain's towns and cities into submission in the hope that Britain would eventually ask for peace.

Germany now turned is attention eastward once again. On September 27, 1940, it signed the Tripartite Pact with its allies Italy and Japan. The three agreed to support one another if they were attacked.

In November, the pact was extended to include Germany's other allies Hungary, Romania, and Slovakia, with Bulgaria joining the following March.

Through this treaty, Germany had access to the oil supplies of Romania, which were crucial for its war effort. It had also secured its southern flank by allying with almost all the Balkan states. It was now almost ready to turn east and face the Soviet Union.

PACT

Article 1. Japan recognizes and respects the leadership of Germany and Italy in the establishment of a new order in Europe.

Article 2. Germany and Italy recognize and respect the leadership of Japan in the establishment of a new order in Greater East Asia.

Article 3. Japan, Germany and Italy agree to cooperate in their efforts on aforesaid lines. They further undertake to assist one another with all political, economic, and military means if one of the Contracting Powers is attacked by a Power at present not involved in the European War or in the Japanese-Chinese conflict.

Article 5. Japan, Germany and Italy affirm that the above agreement affects in no way the political status existing at present between each of the three Contracting Powers and Soviet Russia.

Source: The terms of the Tripartite Pact, September 27, 1940.

The Tripartite Pact made it clear that Germany, Italy, and Japan had divided up Europe and Asia between them. Article 3 became important when Japan attacked the United States on December 7, 1941. Germany and Italy supported Japan and declared war against the U.S. on December 11, even though the U.S. had only declared war on Japan. Article 5 allowed Japan to keep its nonaggression pact with the Soviet Union even after Germany invaded the country in June 1941.

Yugoslavia and Greece

Events, however, were not all going Hitler's way in 1940–41. Germany's ally, Italy, had expanded its power in the Mediterranean by occupying the small Balkan state of Albania in April 1939. It had also attacked British-controlled Egypt in September 1940, although the British had easily repelled its forces. Italy now turned its attention south toward Greece. It accused the Greeks of supporting the British, and demanded the right to use Greek ports and airports to support its campaign in

The main German source of oil to support its armies in the Balkans, and later the Soviet Union, came from the Ploesti oil fields and refineries in Romania. In 1943 and in early 1944, U.S. bombers attacked the refineries to stop production, but without great success. Eventually, they fell to the Soviet Red Army in August 1944.

North Africa. When Greece refused, Italian troops invaded the country from Albania in October 1940.

The Greeks, however, were tough fighters and within a month had expelled the Italians and invaded southern Albania. Hitler was disgusted with his ally's poor performance, but he threatened Greece by marching German troops right up to the Greek border through Bulgaria, after the latter joined the Tripartite Pact on March 1, 1941. Hitler put pressure on Yugoslavia to join the pact, which it did reluctantly on March 25. However, many Yugoslavs had no wish to ally with Germany, and on March 27 overthrew their government and replaced it with a pro-British alternative.

The German response was immediate. Hitler gave orders for *"the destruction of Yugoslavia militarily and as a national unit … [to be] carried out with pitiless harshness."* Together with Bulgaria and Italy, Germany invaded the country on April 6. At the same time, German troops began to pour into Greece.

The Yugoslavs were caught unprepared and agreed an armistice 11 days later. The Greeks kept fighting with British support but eventually lost control of their mainland by May 3, and the southerly island of Crete by the end of the month. With the whole of the Balkans now under German or Italian rule or control, Hitler was ready to face the Soviet Union and its Red Army.

SOURCE

SPEECH

"I could not make a decision to sell my own house on a few hours' notice. How do you expect me to sell my country?"

The Greek response to Italian threats in October 1940 was dismissive.

Greek prime minister General Ioannis Metaxas to Count Emmanuele Grazzi, Italian minister in Athens, October 28, 1940.

The Germans marched about half a million troops into Greece, yet suffered only 5,500 killed or wounded. They surrounded and captured 270,000 Greek troops. This photo shows German troops marching into Greece in 1941.

Operation Barbarossa

It is commonly believed that the German invasion of the Soviet Union was delayed from its planned date in early May to late June 1941 because of the German invasion of Yugoslavia and Greece. The truth, however, is that the late Soviet winter that year meant that the ground was still very muddy until mid-June, so the attack could not have taken place until it dried out. The plan was for three massive armies to invade the Soviet Union—Army Group North to Leningrad, Army Group Center to the capital Moscow, and Army Group South into Ukraine, the granary of the Soviet Union (the Ukraine provided the Soviet Union with grain). Army Group South would then move on to the Caucasus and its oil wells. The invasion was codenamed "Operation Barbarossa" after the medieval German emperor, Frederick Barbarossa, who led the Third Crusade against the Muslims in the 1180s. Hitler saw the invasion as a modern-day crusade of European civilization against "heathen" Slavs, Bolsheviks, and Jews.

The scale of the invasion was breathtaking—it involved 3.6 million

Soviet front-line troops were taken totally by surprise by the invasion, and recived conflicting instructions from their military commanders and their political leaders in Moscow.

men, 3,600 tanks, 2,700 aircraft, 600,000 motor vehicles, and 750,000 horses. The German army put 148 divisions into battle, alongside 14 Romanian and 22 Finnish divisions— fighting to regain territory seized by the Soviet Union in 1940—three Italian and one Slovakian division. Against them would be ranged a much larger Red Army, with 5.5 million men, 20,000 tanks, and 10,000 aircraft. However, the Red Army was disorganized and lacked modern machines.

The attack began at 3:15 a.m. on June 22, 1941. After a short artillery burst, the *Luftwaffe* attacked Soviet airbases, destroying 1,800 aircraft on the ground during the first raid and another 700 a few hours later, with minimal German losses. Then the three armies attacked on a 500-mile front. Many German troops welcomed the invasion of the Soviet Union. Wolfgang Horn, a German soldier remembered " … *a great feeling about the power being unleashed against the dubious and despicable enemy.*"The question, however, is why were the Soviets so unprepared? In January 1941, the Soviet Union had renewed the Nazi-Soviet Pact, although it was concerned about the German military presence in

Finland and Romania. The German military buildup in Poland was hard to hide, and intelligence reports from the British and from Richard Sorge, a German journalist who spied for the

Many of the major battles of Operation Barbarossa were fought by tanks, such as this confrontation in 1941 on the Eastern Front. German tanks were initially superior, but they were no match for the Soviet T-34, which came into service during 1941.

Soviet Union in Tokyo, warned of the forthcoming invasion. A complete set of plans was sent from spies in Switzerland on June 18, stating that the invasion was set to begin in four days. Stalin continued to believe that the pact would hold, and exports of grain and oil to Germany in return for machine tools continued until the morning of the invasion. The Soviets were unprepared and did not want to provoke war.

To the outskirts of Moscow

The first weeks of the campaign saw the Germans inflict massive losses. The *Luftwaffe* virtually wiped out the Red Air Force in the west of the Soviet Union and the rapid thrust of the Panzer (armored) divisions had taken captive or killed more than 600,000 Red Army troops. However, the Soviets fought back with great determination, causing 100,000 German casualties.

At first, Hitler and his generals were anxious to take Moscow and made this their main objective. Hitler believed that Stalin would sacrifice everything to

SOURCE

RADIO BROADCAST

Stalin called for a scorched-earth policy toward the invading German army:

Leave not "*a single railway carriage, a single wagon, a single pound of grain*" for the enemy.

Radio broadcast from Moscow, July 3, 1941.

defend his capital and that this was therefore the best way to defeat the Red Army. On July 19, however, Hitler decided that Leningrad and Ukraine were the main objectives for economic reasons, and he left Moscow to be

bombed into submission by the *Luftwaffe.* Two months later, Hitler once again put Moscow at the center of his plans.

This swapping around caused considerable delays, as equipment was moved from one front to the other and back again. By the end of September, the Army Group Center still had 200 miles (320 km) to go to Moscow, and the fall rains had begun. The Germans then launched a massive assault on the capital. Stalin responded by placing General Georgi Zhukov in charge of its defense. Zhukov ordered three semicircles of defensive ditches to be dug to the west of the city. He brought in reinforcements from Siberia and strengthened the defending army to 578,000 men.

The German occupation of the Soviet Union reached its peak in the fall of 1942, when its armies surrounded Leningrad in the north, and threatened Stalingrad and the Caucasus Mountains in the south.

As the Germans advanced, their progress slowed, held up by seasonal mud, poor supplies, and lack of fuel for their tanks. In mid-November, the rain turned to snow and the ground froze. These conditions suited the Germans better and they advanced to within 20 miles (32 km) of the city center. But on the night of December 4,

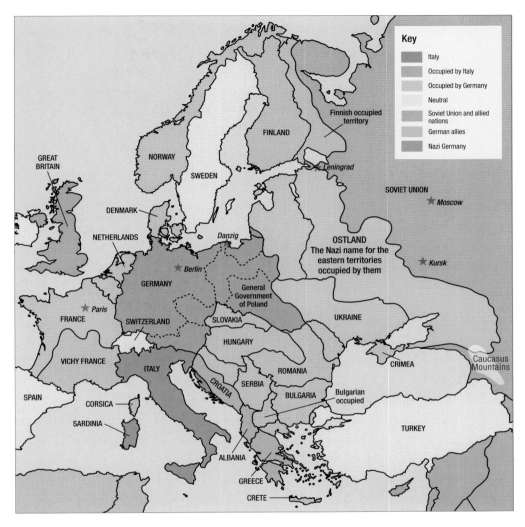

Key

- Italy
- Occupied by Italy
- Occupied by Germany
- Neutral
- Soviet Union and allied nations
- German allies
- Nazi Germany

GREAT BRITAIN

NORWAY

SWEDEN

FINLAND

Finnish occupied territory

Leningrad

SOVIET UNION

★ *Moscow*

DENMARK

NETHERLANDS

Danzig

★ *Berlin*

GERMANY

OSTLAND
The Nazi name for the eastern territories occupied by them

★ *Kursk*

General Government of Poland

FRANCE

★ *Paris*

SWITZERLAND

SLOVAKIA

UKRAINE

HUNGARY

VICHY FRANCE

ITALY

CROATIA

SERBIA

ROMANIA

CRIMEA

Caucasus Mountains

SPAIN

CORSICA

BULGARIA

Bulgarian occupied

SARDINIA

TURKEY

ALBANIA

GREECE

CRETE

the temperature dropped to -31°F. Tank engines would not start, weapons froze, and the troops, wearing clothing unsuited to the severe Soviet winter, soon suffered from frostbite. The attack on the city was called off that evening. Just as "General Winter" had defeated Napoleon and the French army in 1812, it defeated the Germans in the same way 129 years later.

The Red Army then launched a

This map shows the German occupation of the Soviet Union reaching its maximum extent in the fall of 1942. By the spring, the Germans had been pushed back by the Soviet troops.

massive counterattack against German lines. By the fall of 1942, the Germans had been pushed back 100 miles (160 km) from the city. Moscow had been saved, and hundreds of other towns and villages liberated. The costs to both sides had been huge.

The siege of Leningrad

In June and July 1941, the German Army Group North raced up through the Baltic states of Lithuania and Latvia, occupying Estonia by the end of August. In all three states, the Germans were greeted as liberators, since the three had been occupied by the Soviet Union the previous year. By September 11, German troops were within 7.5 miles (12 km) of their target, Leningrad. To the north, their Finnish allies moved south. On September 15, Leningrad was surrounded and cut off from the rest of the country, except by boat across Lake Ladoga.

Yet at this moment orders came through from Hitler to divert resources south to the assault on Moscow. Leningrad was spared a direct German attack, but now prepared to withstand a lengthy siege. Under the control of General Zhukov—soon to direct the defense of Moscow—its citizens dug trenches, built gun emplacements, erected antitank obstacles, and mined bridges and factories ready to be blown up if the Germans tried to storm their way into the city.

The main problem the citizens of Leningrad faced was lack of food. The only roads and railroad lines into the city had been blocked. Supplies had to be flown in to a small airport some 50 miles (80 km) away, then carried by road and by boat across Lake Ladoga. Since rations were cut to about one-sixth of the amount required by a normal healthy person, many people began to die of starvation and disease.

The onset of winter, however, brought some relief to the city as Lake Ladoga froze over. Trucks could now carry food and other much-needed supplies across the ice and bring out refugees and the injured in order to take some of the pressure off the city. By January 1942, 400 trucks a day were shuttling back and forth across the frozen lake.

The city was saved, but it had to endure these terrible conditions for another two years. A pipeline laid across the floor of the lake brought in much-needed fuel, and boats—or trucks in winter—continued to ferry in the necessary supplies.

By the time the siege was lifted on January 19, 1944, the city had endured almost 900 days of hell, with the loss of perhaps 1.5 million lives. Vera Inber, a citizen of Leningrad, recorded the effects of the siege in her diary on December 26, 1941: "*The mortuary itself is full. Not only are there too few trucks to go to the cemetery, but more importantly, not enough gasoline to put in the trucks and the main thing is—there is not enough strength in the living to bury the dead.*"

SYMPHONY

In the early days of the German siege of Leningrad, Dmitry Shostakovich worked as a firefighter putting out fires caused by the German bombardment. His experiences in the city led to the composition of his seventh Leningrad symphony.

The composer, Dmitry Shostakovich (1906–75), was born in St. Petersburg (as Leningrad is now known) and composed his seventh symphony—which he subtitled the *Leningrad Symphony*—during the siege. He wanted the Leningrad Philharmonic Orchestra to perform its world premiere in the city itself, but they had been evacuated, making this impossible. Instead, Moscow's Bolshoi Theater Orchestra performed the premiere in Siberia on March 5, 1942; this was broadcast nationwide and abroad to great acclaim. The Leningrad premiere took place on August 9, 1942. The city was still under siege, and the only musicians available were the 40 to 50 members of the Radio Orchestra. Extra musicians were brought back from the front line and all were given special rations while they rehearsed. Immediately preceding the performance, German gun positions were attacked so that they did not interrupt the concert. Leningrad's Philharmonic Hall was packed for the concert, which was broadcast on loudspeakers throughout the city, and as a propaganda exercise, to German troops continuing the siege.

Under occupation

As the German troops entered the Soviet Union in June 1941 and raced through Ukraine, Belarus, and the Baltic states, many towns and villages welcomed them as liberators from Soviet oppression. Ukraine had suffered a terrible famine during the 1930s, after Stalin tried to take all the farms into state ownership, and some seven million peasant farmers had died. Many Ukrainians believed that the Germans had brought them freedom and independence, and collaborated with them.

Some Soviet prisoners of war (POWs) even changed sides to fight with the Germans as *Hiwis—Hilfswillige*, or "voluntary helpers." The Germans, however, failed to grasp the significance of these events, or indeed use them to their advantage. The Nazis considered Ukrainians, Soviets, and others to be subhuman Slavs whose lives were worthless. Many people who welcomed the Germans in 1941 came to regret their decision later.

German policy toward occupied Eastern Europe was brutal. Poland and Yugoslavia were wiped off the map altogether. Western Poland was absorbed directly into *Grossdeutsches Reich* (Greater Germany), and Yugoslavia was split between German rule in Serbia under the "puppet"

regime of General Nedic and the puppet pro-Nazi Ustase regime of Croatia under German and Italian control. Elsewhere, German military or civilian rule replaced the old governments, and the new dictators ruled their new lands with an iron fist.

SOURCE

SPEECH

"Henceforth 100 prisoners or hostages to be shot for every soldier killed and 50 for every one wounded. Every regional garrison to arrest as many communists, nationalists, democrats, and Jews as possible…"

The Germans kept a tight control over the lands they occupied, as shown by this order from the German High Command to its army in Serbia, Yugoslavia, in October 1941.

Nazi policy toward Poland and the Soviet Union was particularly harsh. These lands were the *lebensraum* (see page 5), and only Germans could be allowed to prosper there. As the German army advanced eastward, action groups of SS *Einsatzgruppen* troops followed it, exterminating all enemies of the Nazi state, particularly

Jews and communists.

Countless thousands lost their lives to these death squads, and many people were evicted from their homes and farms to make way for German settlers. Millions more lost their lives as they became caught up in battle or were besieged and bombarded in towns. German troops stole crops and livestock, food, clothes, and other household items and burned down homes. Countless numbers in the east died in the bitter Soviet winter of 1941.

SOURCE

PROPAGANDA POSTER

This U.S. propaganda poster refers to events that took place in May 1942. After two Czech partisans assassinated Reinhard Heydrich, the tyrannical Nazi ruler of western Czechoslovakia, the Germans responded by murdering all the men in the village of Lidice, where the partisans lived, and in nearby Lezaky. They deported the women and children to Ravensbrück concentration camp. More than 5,000 were killed in revenge for Heydrich's death.

This is Nazi brutality

RADIO BERLIN.--IT IS OFFICIALLY ANNOUNCED:- ALL MEN OF LIDICE - CZECHOSLOVAKIA - HAVE BEEN SHOT: THE WOMEN DEPORTED TO A CONCENTRATION CAMP: THE CHILDREN SENT TO APPROPRIATE CENTERS-- THE NAME OF THE VILLAGE WAS IMMEDIATELY ABOLISHED. 6/11/42/115P

The Jews

Of all the people who lived in Eastern Europe, the Jews had the most to fear from the Nazis. The Nazis were fiercely anti-Semitic and considered Jews to be subhuman. They wanted to clear all Jews out of Europe by any means. At first, that meant encouraging Jewish emigration from Germany to whichever countries would take them. As Nazi rule was extended across most of Europe, this became impractical, so they adopted far more brutal tactics.

The invasion and occupation of western Poland brought 2.25 million Jews under German rule. Many managed to flee eastward into the Soviet Union, but thousands were shot on the spot or rounded up by the *Einsatzgruppen* death squads and herded into walled or fenced ghettos in the poor parts of towns. There, their food rations were cut and medical supplies restricted, leading to numerous deaths from hunger and disease. Many more Jews were sent to labor camps, where they worked—often to death—producing materials needed for the German war effort, such as cement, oil, and rubber.

SOURCE

PROPAGANDA POSTER

This is a German anti-Jewish propaganda poster from 1942 with the word *Winniza* (the name of a town in the Ukraine). It shows a Jewish political officer from the Soviet Red Army looming over the war dead of the town and their grieving widows and mothers. The implication was that the Jews working with the Red Army were responsible for the war and its brutal consequences.

At this stage of the war, Nazi policy toward the Jews was confused, since they had no clear idea what to do about the large numbers under their control. The invasion of the Soviet Union in June 1941 made this problem far worse. There were now up to three million Jews in the Soviet Union and they would have to be dealt with if the invasion was to be successful. Although the *Einsatzgruppen* were efficient and brutal— many Jews were forced to dig mass graves into which they were shot —the Nazis could not cope with disposing of such vast numbers of people.

At a high-level Nazi conference at Wannsee outside Berlin in January 1942, the decision was taken to transport all European Jews by train to the east and kill them in specially built death camps. Five of these were constructed, the most notorious of which was Auschwitz in southern Poland. At least 1.6 million Jews were killed in these camps, and millions more were worked to death in labor camps, starved in ghettos, or shot.

For the Jews, life under the Nazis was hellish and there was almost no escape. However, when the Germans began to close the Warsaw ghetto in April 1943 and deport its inhabitants to the death camps, the Jews rose in revolt. The Germans retaliated by burning down the ghetto building by building. Within a month, 56,000 Jews had been killed or deported, but 15,000 had managed to escape to join the Polish resistance.

Across Europe, Jews were forced to labor for the Nazis, building fortifications and roads or clearing bomb damage. These people were all inhabitants of the Warsaw ghetto, set up in November 1940 to incarcerate the city's Jews.

SOURCE

SPEECH

"Today I will once more be a prophet: if the international Jewish financiers in and outside Europe should succeed in plunging the nations once more into a world war, then the result will not be the Bolshevization of the Earth and thus the victory of Jewry, but the annihilation of the Jewish race in Europe."

Adolf Hitler, January 30, 1939.

The battle for Stalingrad

One of the most important and decisive battles of WWII took place in and around Stalingrad in southern Russia. The battle raged from June 1942 to February 1943. The victory or defeat of either side in the whole world war depended on the outcome of this battle.

After their failure to knock the Soviet Union out of the war in 1941, the Germans returned to battle in summer 1942. Their plan—codenamed "Operation Blue"—was to invade and occupy the southern Soviet Union to gain control of the Caucasus oilfields. The plan included the capture of Stalingrad. The city was situated on the Volga River and was the center from which the railroad and waterway communications of the south were controlled. Along these routes, oil from the Caspian Sea was transported north to supply the Red Army. On August 19, the German 6th Army attacked the city from the northwest and the 4th Panzer Army from the southwest. By September 12, the two armies had entered the suburbs and squeezed the Soviets into a 30-mile (48-km) perimeter zone on the west bank of the Volga. During the next two months, the Germans bombarded most of the city to rubble as they slowly pushed the Soviets back into a strip of industrial land along the river's edge.

The battle for Stalingrad was ferocious. The two sides were often so close to each other that they fought each other from different stories of the

The battle for Stalingrad took place amid the ruined houses and factories of the industrial town, with huge loss of life on both sides.

same building. Soviet snipers hid in the rubble and picked off German attackers one by one: a sniper reaching 40 kills gained a "for bravery" medal and the title of "noble sniper."

As the Germans slowly moved in to capture the city, the Red Army launched a surprise counterattack—codenamed "Operation Uranus'—on November 19 behind the German lines. Four days later, the Germans were themselves surrounded. The besieging army was now under siege itself. This double siege of the Soviet city and German army continued into the new year. The stakes for both sides were immense: Stalin had to win the battle for the city named after him, and Hitler could not be defeated in the city named after his main enemy.

In December, the Germans tried but failed to rescue their trapped army, and the Soviet offer of surrender terms was refused in January by Hitler. Worn out by hunger, cold, and constant Soviet attacks, the German 6th Army under General Paulus eventually surrendered on February 2. Over 94,000 troops surrendered with him, but at least 200,000 troops had already died. Of those who surrendered, fewer than 10,000 ever returned to their home. The myth of German invincibility was now shattered.

RADIO MESSAGE

"Attacks in undiminished violence … frightful conditions in the city area proper where about 20,000 unattended wounded are seeking shelter among the ruins. With them are about the same number of starved and frostbitten men, and stragglers."

Conditions inside Stalingrad were appalling as shown by this radio message from the German 6th Army HQ trapped in Stalingrad to HQ Army Group Don, January 24, 1943.

LEAFLET

During the battle for Stalingrad, both sides used propaganda leaflets to undermine the enemy's will to fight. This Soviet leaflet—written in German and issued in January 1943, just before the final German surrender—tells the German troops how many of them have already been taken prisoner.

6500 Soldaten und Offiziere wurden gefangengenommen. Insgesamt wurden seit dem 19. November 1942 von den Sowjettruppen

**144 150 deutsche Soldaten und Offiziere
gefangengenommen.**

In der Zeit vom 1. bis zum 5. Januar 1943 wurden
vernichtet:
88 deutsche Flugzeuge, 118 Panzer, 122 Ge-
schütze verschiedenen Kalibers, 291 Granatwerfer,
787 MG., 570 Kfz. mit Truppen und Heeresgut,
340 Krafträder, 432 Eisenbahnwaggons und 20 ver-
schiedene Lager.

In der Zeit vom 1. bis zum 5. Januar 1943 verlor
der Gegner allein an Toten mehr als 20 000 Soldaten und Offiziere.

Das Informationsbüro der Sowjetunion

The Battle of Kursk

After the German defeat at Stalingrad, the Soviets began the lengthy task of recapturing land lost to the Germans in the west of the Soviet Union. Twenty months into the war, the Red Army had reorganized and re-equipped itself, mastering new tactics with which to fight. Attacks now began with a heavy artillery bombardment against German lines, during which small attacks by infantry supported by tanks probed any weaknesses. When these were discovered, large numbers of tanks would then pour into the gap, breaking through German lines and forcing their retreat. The Red Army often used deception to surprise the enemy and coordinated their attacks with partisans operating behind German lines (see pages 36–37).

They also developed a system of "rolling offensives": as one offensive began to run out of momentum, another would be launched elsewhere.

All these new tactics were put into operation at Kursk in the Soviet Union. The city had been captured by the Germans in October 1941 and was only recaptured by the Red Army in February 1943. This created a huge Soviet "salient," or bulge, that jutted westward into German lines. The Soviets had reinforced this salient with circular defensive lines of different sizes, but the Germans decided to remove the salient and straighten out their own front line. Despite their defeat at Stalingrad, the German army was still powerful and in no mood to retreat.

In the first stage of "Operation Citadel," the massive battle to remove the Kursk salient, German tanks advanced to the city from the north and south on July 4, 1943. The devastation wrought by the tanks of both sides can be clearly seen in this photograph.

The German attack began on July 4, with massive air and artillery bombardments. The German force was vast with 900,000 men, 2,700 tanks, and 2,000 aircraft. However, the Red Army was now much stronger, with 1,300,000 men and 3,000 tanks. To the north of the city, the Germans advanced only 4 miles (6.5 km) on the first day; to the south, the advance was 9 miles (14.5 km). Slowly but surely, the Red Army stopped the German assault.

SOURCE

PROPAGANDA POSTER

This Soviet propaganda poster from 1943 makes it very clear who is winning the war, as a single Red Army soldier kills a group of Germans while the Red Flag flies in the background.

The Red Army was now ready to attack. On July 12, a massive tank battle took place near the village of Prokhorovka, south of Kursk. In what is the biggest tank battle in history, 850 Soviet tanks fought 600 German tanks at almost point-blank range. At least 700 tanks were knocked out, with enormous casualties—more than 250,000 troops lost their lives during the entire 10-day battle—but the Germans were beaten. The next day they called off the attack and the Red Army went on the offensive.

The Red Army advances

The victory at Kursk coincided with the Allied invasion of Italy and the country's surrender two months later. Hitler now had to fight on two fronts, since German troops were required in Italy to prevent the entire country from falling into Allied hands. The Red Army seized the initiative and pressed westward into Ukraine. As it advanced, its confidence and strength grew daily.

Although they had been caught off guard by the German attack, the Soviets soon put their economy onto a total war footing. This meant that

factories situated well behind the front line in the Ural Mountains, between Europe and Asia, began to produce thousands of tanks, airplanes, artillery pieces, guns, trucks, and other war materials. The Red Army was reorganized and received proper training, and it began to gain a resolute fighting spirit. Buoyed up by their victories at Stalingrad and Kursk, the Red Army was now ready to go on the offensive.

The scale of the Soviet attack westward toward the Dneiper River was

As the Red Army pushed westward through Ukraine during 1943, it encountered wrecked villages and many near-starving people. Most of the roads were little better than mud tracks, churned up by tanks and armored vehicles into marshy quagmires.

immense. More than 2,630,000 men, 51,000 guns and mortars, 2,400 tanks, and 2,850 aircraft were organized into five vast armies. They faced the Germans, who had 1,240,000 men, 12,600 guns and mortars, 2,100 tanks, and 2,100 aircraft. The Soviets therefore had twice as many men and four times as much artillery, but not many more tanks and aircraft. The Soviet plan was to cross the Dnieper, and in the north, retake the Ukrainian capital, Kiev. The battle began on August 13 along a 400-mile (645-km) front and continued until December. By then, the Red Army had successfully crossed the river, retaken Kiev and 160 other towns and cities, and moved 100 miles (160 km) farther to the west.

If the second half of 1943 had seen massive Soviet victories at Kursk and Kiev, the first half of 1944 saw huge Soviet advances to the north. The siege of Leningrad was lifted in January, the Belorussian capital, Minsk, was taken in early July, and by the end of the month, the Red Army had reached the East Prussian frontier of Germany and pushed into Poland.

The territory gained was immense, but so, too, was the cost to both sides. Stalin was determined to drive the Germans out of the Soviet Union, but Hitler refused to allow any of his troops to withdraw. Hundreds of thousands of troops lost their lives, and 300,000 German prisoners were taken at Minsk alone.

SOURCE

RECOLLECTION

"The men were first-rate fighters from the start ... They became first-rate soldiers with experience. They fought most toughly, had amazing endurance, and could carry on without most of the things other armies regarded as necessities. The [Red Army general] staff were quick to learn from their early defeats, and soon became highly efficient ... Their artillery was excellent, and also most of the infantry weapons— their rifles were more modern than ours, and had a more rapid rate of fire. Their T-34 tank was the finest in the world."

The Red Army developed into a superb fighting force in 1943 and 1944, as even its German opponents recognized.

General Ewald von Kleist, commander of the German First Panzer Army, 1944.

By August 1944, the Red Army had established a line that ran down the eastern borders of the three Baltic states and south through Poland into Romania. Such a rapid advance was extremely difficult to sustain as the supplies ran out, or could not be sent to the front quickly enough to support the troops. This situation was to have catastrophic consequences outside the Polish capital, Warsaw.

The Warsaw Uprising

One of the most controversial events of the war took place in the Polish capital, Warsaw, in August 1944. The Poles had suffered terribly under German occupation and wanted to regain their freedom. With the Red Army only 8 miles (13 km) away across the River Vistula, the *Armija Krajowa*, the AK or Polish Home Army, rose in revolt.

The Home Army had about 40,000 men armed mainly with captured German weapons, with another 210,000 unarmed helpers. However, they had no artillery or tanks, and were no match for the much stronger German army that was determined to hold the city at all costs. The revolt broke out on the afternoon of August 1, and within four days, the Poles had seized three-fifths of their city. However, they had failed to take either the railroad stations or any of the Vistula bridges. The Germans responded with massive force, slowly retaking the city street by street, with unbelievable cruelty. At least 225,000 civilians and 15,000 fighters, lost their lives by the time the city surrendered to the Germans on October 2.

Politically, the uprising was a failure. It had been ordered by the Polish nationalist government-in-exile in London, not to help the Soviet advance, but to forestall it. The government-in-exile saw the liberation of Warsaw as a symbol of the future independence of a democratic Poland. It feared that if the Red Army liberated Warsaw, capital and country would later become communist, which did happen in 1947. Their plans became more urgent when, only days before

German soldiers take shelter in the Warsaw Opera House, during a battle with the Polish Home Army in the Warsaw Uprising of August to October 1944.

German troops captured many members of the Polish
Home Army during the Warsaw Uprising of 1944. The
15,000 Polish fighters who survived the battle were
granted prisoner of war status by the Germans and were
marched off to prison camps after the uprising was over.
This picture shows German soldiers during the uprising.

the uprising on July 21, a communist-backed Polish Committee for National Liberation was set up. It created a provisional government and signed a friendship treaty with the Soviet Union. The Polish leader in exile, Stanislaw Mikolajczyk, then urged immediate action to prevent a communist government taking Warsaw.

The uprising had also been a terrible military mistake, as the Poles did not have enough weapons to expel the Germans. Many people blamed Stalin for not ordering the Red Army to enter the city. But the reality was that the city was beyond its grasp. The Germans put up massive resistance to the Soviet advance in early August, especially near the river crossings. For its part, the Red Army was tired, short of arms, and operating on very extended lines of supply. The rising would have made sense if the Soviets

RADIO BROADCAST

"People of Warsaw, to arms! Attack the Germans! Help the Red Army ... show the way."

Radio broadcasts urged Warsaw to rise up against the Germans.

Polish radio broadcast from Moscow, July 29, 1944.

had been about to enter the city, but that was not the case: they would not capture Warsaw until January 1945.

35

Behind enemy lines

A partisan is a member of an armed resistance group that fights a guerrilla war inside a country against an invading or occupying army. Partisans made a memorable contribution to fighting the Germans in the occupied Soviet Union, but their role was often controversial, and they were sometimes feared as much by their own side as by the enemy.

they hid in the remote forests and marshes in the west of the Soviet Union, Belorussia, and Ukraine. Here they scavenged for food from local people, who were often short of food themselves, and began to form fighting units. Escaping prisoners of war swelled their numbers to at least 300,000 by the end of 1941, but few of them had weapons, communication

The first Soviet partisans were not so much volunteers as unwilling victims of circumstance. As the German army swept eastward, thousands of Red Army soldiers, Communist Party officials, and Jews were caught behind German lines. Fearful of what the Germans would do to them if they were caught,

This is a Soviet propaganda poster from July 13, 1941. It celebrates a partisan unit surrounding and attacking German soldiers, who are in the process of plundering a Soviet farm and taking its workers captive.

radios, medical supplies, and other necessities. The partisans were facing a much better equipped enemy and lived in constant fear of German reprisals. On September 16, 1941, the Germans announced that between 50 and 100 partisans would be executed for every German soldier killed.

In May 1942, Stalin set up the "Central Staff for Partisan Warfare" to coordinate partisan activities. Supplies of guns, heavy artillery, and even tanks and airplanes were provided, and military experts were parachuted in to train and organize the various groups. By 1943, the partisans were taking a huge toll on the German army, attacking supply convoys, blowing up railroad lines and bridges, and assassinating individual Germans, including Wilhelm Kube, the German commissar of Belorussia who was blown up by a time bomb placed under his bed by a partisan maid.

Not all partisans were fighting for the Soviet Union, however. Many Ukrainian partisans were nationalists fighting for independence from both German and Soviet rule. By 1943, around 300,000 Ukrainian nationalists were creating havoc against both sides, some fighting after the Soviet re-occupation of Ukraine in 1943–44 until the late 1940s. In other places, the partisans were little better than

This Soviet postcard from 1943 celebrates the hero paritsans with the words "to the New Year," *and* "may the terrible lightning of the people's anger strike and thunder loudly, just as the thunder of the sublime words of vengeance!"

brigands, stealing food and goods from local people and executing anyone they suspected of collaboration with the Germans. Many partisans were betrayed to the Germans by local people anxious to safeguard their own lives. The Soviet partisan oath was to *"work a terrible, merciless and unrelenting revenge against the enemy. ... Blood for blood! Death for death!"*

Liberating the Balkans

The Balkans are the countries situated on the southeastern peninsula of Europe (see map on page 21). During the war, the situation here was politically and militarily confused. Fascist or authoritarian governments modeled on Nazi Germany and fascist Italy controlled Slovakia, Hungary, Romania, and Bulgaria. All four were allies of Germany, and from 1940–41, signatories to the Tripartite Pact with Italy and Japan against the Soviet Union. They supported Germany out of economic and political self-interest; Romanian and Slovakian troops took part in the German invasion of the U.S.S.R. However, Germany had rearranged the Romanian borders to reward Bulgaria and Hungary, compensating Romania with land taken from the Soviet Union. Political maneuverings like this meant that relations between the four allies and Germany were often tense.

In the early years of the war, these countries benefited economically and politically from their German alliance, but they became worried as the tide of war turned against Germany after the Battle for Stalingrad. As the Red Army headed into Romania in August 1944, King Michael I deposed the fascist dictator, Ion Antonescu, ordered the Romanian army to stop fighting and declared war on Germany. A month later, Bulgaria changed sides as well.

After the occupation of Romania by the Red Army in August 1944, the Soviet Union declared war on neighboring Bulgaria and occupied the country on September 8. The old pro-German government was quickly ousted by a pro-Soviet government, which promptly declared war on Germany. Bulgarians rejoiced in their liberation from fascist rule.

4

The situation in Hungary was complicated by the refusal of the Hungarian government to hand over the country's 800,000 Jews for extermination by the Germans. As a result, Germany occupied the country in March 1944. German troops also occupied Slovakia in August 1944, after resistance fighters in league with the

Italian military rule, although the Yugoslav province of Croatia was semi-independent under its own fascist government. Albania had, since 1939, been united with Italy. German troops had replaced the Italians in the three countries after the surrender of Italy in September 1943, and now found themselves massively overstretched.

The headquarters of the partisans in the mountains near Dvrar in western Bosnia were well camouflaged and defended against possible German attack.

Slovak army threatened to overthrow the pro-German government and fight with the approaching Soviets. A massive uprising broke out, which was crushed with great severity by the German troops.

The rapid Soviet advance into the southern Balkans threatened German troops in the region. After the German invasion of April 1941, Yugoslavia and Greece had been under German or

German troops had to withdraw from Greece in November 1944 and were expelled from Albania by the communist partisans of Enver Hoxha. The incoming Red Army jointly liberated Belgrade, the capital, in October and most northern parts of the country by the end of the year.

Into Germany

On January 1, 1945—the start of the last year of the war—Allied armies surrounded Germany. The Soviets had liberated their own territory and reached the eastern German frontier in East Prussia. From there, the front line between the Red Army and German troops ran south around the eastern outskirts of Warsaw and down across Poland, Hungary, and Yugoslavia to the Adriatic Sea. In the south, Allied armies had reached northern Italy, and in the west, Allied armies had landed in Normandy on D-Day in June 1944. They had liberated France and Belgium and were poised to cross the Rhine into Germany.

On February 2, 1945, the three Allied leaders—Josef Stalin of the Soviet Union, Winston Churchill of Britain, and President Roosevelt of the United States—met at the Black Sea resort of Yalta in the Crimean peninsula. They agreed that a defeated Germany would be divided between the four main Allied powers—the Soviet Union, the U.S., Britain, and France—with the German capital, Berlin, divided between all four, too. Crucially, this division meant that Berlin fell inside the Soviet zone. The road to Berlin and final victory over Nazi Germany now lay open to the advancing Red Army.

The final offensive against Germany had actually begun on January 12, when Red Army troops crossed the Vistula River south of Warsaw and headed west across Poland. Warsaw fell to the Soviets on January 17 and by February 3, the Red Army had established bridgeheads across the

SOURCE

RECOLLECTION

"Troops of the 1st Polish Army treat Germans especially severely. Often captured German officers and soldiers do not reach prisoner assembly areas. They are shot en route. For example, on the sector ... 80 Germans were captured. Just two prisoners reached the assembly area."

Both Soviets and Poles treated captured German troops very harshly.

General Serov, chief of the NKVD—Soviet secret police—with the 1st Belorussian Front Red Army.

Oder River, the last major obstacle to Berlin and only 40 miles (64 km) from the capital itself. As the Red Army rapidly advanced, tales of mass rape, murder, and plunder traveled ahead of them. Many troops wanted to avenge the devastation the Germans had caused in their country, but others just wanted extra food and beverages, and some new warm, dry clothes and boots. Polish troops fighting with the Soviets had the reputation of being even more savage toward the German people.

As a result of the advancing Red Army and the savagery that some of these soldiers brought with them, millions of Germans fled their homes in East Prussia and Poland for what they thought would be relative safety in the heart of Germany. Many chose to flee west in ships, only to find that they were then torpedoed by Soviet submarines in the Baltic Sea. In the greatest maritime loss in history, the *Wilhelm Gustloff* set sail from Gdynia in Poland on January 30 with 10,582 passengers. It was torpedoed and sank, losing all but 1,300 lives.

SOURCE

MILITARY ORDER

On April 23, 1945, as the Red Army closed in on Berlin, Hitler issued orders (below) to the 12th Army, commanded by General Wenck and currently fighting U.S. troops on the River Elbe to the west, to come to the defense of the city: *"The Hun Storm of genocidal Bolshevism must be destroyed before the walls of the Reich capital…"* In reality, however, Wenck wanted to open up a route to allow German soldiers and civilians to escape both the fighting and the ruthless Red Army, and flee westward toward the more humane U.S. troops.

Soldaten der Armee Wenck!

Ein Befehl von größter Tragweite hat Euch aus Euren Aufmarschräumen gegen unsere westlichen Feinde herausgerufen und in Richtung nach Osten in Marsch gesetzt. Euer Auftrag ist klar:

Berlin bleibt deutsch!

Der Hunnensturm des völkervernichtenden Bolschewismus muß vor und in den Mauern der Reichshauptstadt zerschlagen werden.

Der Führer steht an der Spitze der Verteidigung Berlins.

Er hat Eurem tapferen Oberbefehlshaber mitgeteilt, daß er im Vertrauen auf Euer schnelles und entschlossenes Eingreifen mit Zuversicht der Entscheidungsschlacht um Berlin entgegensieht.

Soldaten der Armee Wenck!

Nicht nur der Führer, ganz Berlin wartet und hofft

...dt wird schon

The fall of Berlin

In order to protect Berlin from the advancing Red Army, Hitler ordered the construction of two, or in places, three massive defensive lines. These consisted of tank traps, gun positions, and other defenses that stretched from the Baltic Sea 200 miles (320 km) south along the Oder and Neisse rivers to the Sudeten mountains in the south. However, the one million German soldiers protecting this line faced at least 2.5 million better-equipped and better-motivated Soviet troops.

The main attack began on April 16 with a massive bombardment against German positions on the Selow Heights, the main obstacle on the direct road west to Berlin. Marshal Zhukov's 1st Belorussian Front Army opened fire with one gun for every 13 feet (4 km) of the 55-mile (90-km) front line. As they moved west to Berlin, a second large army—the 1st Ukrainian Front under Marshal Koniev—swept up toward Berlin from the southeast, and a third army—the 2nd Belorussian Front under Marshal Rokossovsky—headed north of Berlin toward the Baltic ports.

On April 24, Zhukov's and Koniev's armies met southwest of Berlin, circling the city with Soviet troops. The next day, Soviet troops and U.S. troops met at Torgau on the River Elbe. East and west had now met and Germany

SOURCE

ARMY INSTRUCTION

As the Red Army occupied Berlin, its High Command issued an instruction (left) in German: *"A call to the people of Berlin to assist the Soviet military authorities in the fight against Nazi leaders."* Most Berliners, however, were too frightened or demoralized to turn on their former rulers.

was divided in two.

The final battle for the city of Berlin began on April 26 with a massive bombardment.

Half a million Soviet troops supported by 12,700 pieces of artillery and 21,000 multiple rocket launchers attacked the city center.

The devastation was massive, as German soldiers fought to protect Hitler and the Nazi Third Reich from final defeat. The final battle took place around the *Reichstag* (parliament) building on April 30: 5,000 SS and other troops fought for every floor and stairway until they were finally overcome. The same day, Hitler committed suicide in his underground bunker 220 yards (200 m) away. One by one, German armies began to surrender until, at 2:41 a.m. on May 7,

*This famous photograph of Red Army sergeants Yegorov and Kantariya raising the Red Flag over the **Reichstag** in Berlin, supposedly on April 30, is actually a posed shot. The flag was only placed on the roof much later that evening. Stalin wanted to announce that the **Reichstag** had fallen in time for the Soviet May Day holiday. In reality, the fighting in the building continued until the afternoon of May 1, and the photograph was not taken until the fighting was over.*

a total surrender of German troops was agreed at the headquarters of General Eisenhower, the Supreme Commander of the Allied Forces in western Europe, at Rheims in northern France. The war in Europe was over.

The aftermath

At the end of WWII in Europe in May 1945, the continent was divided. Soviet troops occupied Eastern Europe. U.S., British, Canadian, and other Allied troops occupied western Europe. The military division soon became political, too.

In October 1944, Stalin and Churchill had agreed the postwar division of Eastern Europe: Bulgaria, Hungary, Romania, and Yugoslavia fell

In this official photograph, the commander of the U.S. 69th Infantry Division, General Reinhardt, is seen shaking hands with a Soviet general from the 58th Guards Division on April 26 on the River Elbe. In reality, a U.S. patrol had met the Red Army troops the day before, but no photographer was on hand. The postwar division of Germany into east and west was symbolized by this historic meeting.

under communist Soviet influence, and Greece became a democracy. The Yalta Conference of February 1945 (see page 40) brought about the division of postwar Germany and Berlin into four

occupied zones. In 1949, the eastern, Soviet zone became the communist German Democratic Republic with its capital in East Berlin. The three western zones—British, French, and U.S.—formed the democratic German Federal Republic with its capital in Bonn. Austria was divided into four zones and became a democratic state. The four-power occupation ended when troops were withdrawn by agreement in 1955. Stalin insisted that Poland become communist and act as a barrier between the Soviet Union and Germany. He also insisted that the Soviet-Polish border be moved west to follow the line of the 1939 Nazi-Soviet Pact, and that the three Baltic states become part of the Soviet Union. Poland acquired a large part of eastern Germany in compensation.

By 1949, the division of Europe was complete, between the communist east and the democratic west. In Churchill's words, an "*iron curtain*" divided them. The division remained until the fall of communism across Eastern Europe in 1989, the reunification of Germany in 1990, and the final collapse of the communist Soviet Union in 1991.

TIMELINE

1939

August	Nazi-Soviet nonaggression pact agreed.
September	Germany invades Poland.
September	World War II begins as Britain and France declare war on Germany.

1940

March	Winter War between Soviet Union and Finland ends.
April–May	Germany invades Denmark, Norway, Netherlands, Belgium, Luxembourg, and France.
June	The Soviet Union occupies Estonia, Latvia, and Lithuania.
June	France surrenders.
September	Tripartite Pact signed between Germany, Italy, and Japan.
October	Italy invades Greece.
November	Hungary, Romania, and Slovakia join Tripartite Pact.

1941

March	Bulgaria signs Tripartite Pact. Yugoslavia also signs and then repudiates it.
April	Germany invades Yugoslavia and Greece.
May	Crete, the last Greek island, falls under German control.
June	Operation Barbarossa: Germany invades the Soviet Union.
September	Siege of Leningrad begins.
December	Japan attacks U.S. fleet at Pearl Harbor; the United States enters the war on the Allied side.

1943

February	Red Army defeats Germans at Stalingrad.
July	Red Army wins massive tank battle at Kursk.
July	Allies invade Italy.
August	Red Army begins massive offensive into Ukraine.
September	Italy surrenders.

1944

January	Siege of Leningrad lifts.
March	German troops occupy Hungary.
June	D-Day: Allies land on Normandy beaches to begin liberation of France.
July	Red Army takes Minsk and moves into Poland.
August–October	Warsaw Uprising.
October	Moscow Conference between Churchill and Stalin.
October	Tito's partisans and Red Army liberate Belgrade.

1945

January	Red Army begins massive offensive in Poland.
January	Red Army finally liberates Warsaw.
February	Allied leaders meet at Yalta, Crimea.
February	Red Army takes Budapest, Hungary.
April	Soviet attack across the Oder and Neisse rivers into Germany.
April	Red Army surrounds and then attacks Berlin city center.
May	Germany surrenders.
August	U.S. drops atomic bomb on Hiroshima; Japan surrenders.

GLOSSARY

Allies
A coalition of countries against Nazi Germany and its allies in World War II, including the U.S., Britain, and the Soviet Union.

Annex
To acquire territory through conquest or occupation.

Anti-Semitism
Prejudice against the Jews.

Appeasement
Foreign policy that tries to soothe or calm an enemy by agreeing to some of the demands in the hope of averting war.

Armistice
Agreement between opposing sides to a cease-fire while a peace agreement is reached.

Artillery
Heavy guns such as cannon, mortars, and howitzers.

Authoritarian
A political system where obedience to a ruling person or group is enforced.

Bolshevik
A member of the radical communist group that seized power in the Soviet Union in 1917. The Bolsheviks became the Communist Party in 1918.

Brigands
Bandits operating in mountainous areas.

Collaborator
Someone who works with and for the enemy.

Communism
Economic and social system where in theory everyone is equal, and where all property is owned collectively, by the people.

Concentration camp
Prison camp where Jews and others were held in captivity and often worked to death.

Conscription
Compulsory military service or work in industry or civil defense.

Death camp
Also called an extermination camp, where Jews and others were systematically killed, usually by poison gas.

Demilitarized
An area where all weapons and soldiers have been removed after an agreement is made to stop fighting.

Democracy
Government by the people or their elected representatives.

Deport
To expel or remove someone from a country.

Dictator
Leader who takes complete control of a country and often rules by force.

Einsatzgruppen
"Action groups" of SS troops who murdered enemies of the Nazis, notably Jews and communists.

Fascism
Extreme political movement based on nationalism, and usually, military authority that aims to unite a country's people into a disciplined force under an all-powerful leader.

Ghetto
An area of a town where Jews were forced to live.

Guerrilla
Member of an unofficial, usually politically motivated armed force.

Holocaust
Deliberate attempt by the Nazis to kill all Jews in Europe.

Infantry
Foot soldiers.

Labor camp
Work camp using slave labor, mostly Jews and prisoners of war, to produce materials for the German war effort.

Lebensraum
German word for "living space," territory in Eastern Europe into which Germany could expand.

Luftwaffe
German air force.

Nationalist
Person who is passionately loyal to his or her own country.

Nazi Party
Extreme fascist party led by Adolf Hitler that ruled Germany from 1933–45; Nazi is an abbreviation for the National Socialist German Workers' Party.

Neutral
Describes a nation that refuses to take sides in a war and does not fight.

Partisan
Member of an armed resistance group fighting inside a country against an invading or occupying army.

Plunder
To rob a place or people using violence.

Puppet state
One state, in theory independent, but in fact controlled by another.

Red Army
Army of the Soviet Union.

Soviet Union
Union of the Soviet Socialist Republics, commonly known as Russia, a communist state that existed from 1922–91.

SS
Schutzstaffel, or "protection squads," originally Hitler's personal bodyguard but later expanded into a massive organization responsible for killing enemies of the state.

Third Reich
Name given to Nazi rule in Germany; *reich* is German for "empire."

FURTHER INFORMATION

FURTHER READING

Documenting WWII: Battles of World War II by Neil Tong, Rosen Young Adult, 2008

Documenting World War II: Occupation and Resistance by Simon Adams, Rosen Young Adult, 2008

Documenting World War II: The Holocaust by Neil Tong, Rosen Young Adult, 2008

The World Wars: Germany and Japan Attack by Sean Sheehan, Raintree, 2001

World War II by Simon Adams, DK Children, 2007

World War II: The Allied Victory by Sean Sheehan, Wayland, 2000

Web Sites
Due to the changing nature of Internet links, Rosen Publishing has developed an online list of Web Sites related to the subject of this book. This site is regularly updated. Please use this link to access this list:
http://www.rosenlinks.com/dww/eafr

PLACES TO VISIT

The National World War II Museum, 945 Magazine Street, New Orleans, LA 70130

United States Holocaust Memorial Museum, 100 Raoul Wallenberg Place, SW Washington, DC 20024-2126

U.S. Air Force Museum, 1100 Spaatz Street, Wright-Patterson Air Force Base, Ohio 45433

INDEX

Numbers in **bold** refer to illustrations.